I0558346

TEEN STOLEN

FOCUS

Navigating Distractions and Cultivating Resilience: A Journey Through the Digital Age for Teens.

GBOGO .S. ADEGBOYE

Copyright © 2024 Gbogo .S. Adegboye
This item was printed in the United States of
America, all rights reserved. Without prior
written consent, no portion of this book may
be utilized or duplicated, with the exception
of brief quotations that are included in critical
articles or reviews.

INTRODUCTION

In the bustling landscape of the digital age, where smartphones are ubiquitous extensions of our hands, and social media platforms serve as virtual town squares, the adolescent journey has taken on new dimensions. Today's teenagers navigate a world that is both interconnected and infinitely distracting, where the allure of constant stimulation competes with the demands of focus, presence, and genuine connection.

Welcome to "Teens Stolen Focus," a poignant exploration of the challenges faced by today's youth in maintaining their attention amidst the relentless onslaught of digital distractions. In this book, we embark on a journey to unravel the complexities of teenage life in the digital era, shining a light on the pervasive influence of technology on adolescent behavior, mental health, education, and social interactions.

At the heart of our exploration lies a pressing question: How do we reclaim our focus in a world designed to capture our attention at every turn? Through thought-provoking insights, real-life stories, and practical strategies, "Teens Stolen Focus" endeavors to equip teenagers, parents, educators, and policymakers with the tools and knowledge needed to navigate the digital landscape with intentionality, resilience, and mindfulness.
In the pages that follow, we delve into the multifaceted facets of the digital dilemma, from the impact of excessive screen time on mental health to the challenges of maintaining focus in the classroom and fostering meaningful relationships amidst the digital noise. We confront the reality of digital addiction and its far-reaching consequences, while also celebrating the resilience and potential of today's youth to rise above the distractions and reclaim their focus.

As we embark on this journey together, let us not succumb to despair in the face of overwhelming digital distractions, but rather embrace the opportunity to cultivate a more mindful and balanced approach to technology use. Through collective effort and conscious awareness, we can empower our teenagers to thrive in the digital age, reclaiming their focus and forging meaningful connections in a world brimming with endless possibilities. Join us as we embark on a transformative exploration of "Teens Stolen Focus," where the journey toward reclaiming our attention begins with a single page turn.

This introduction sets the stage for the book, framing the discussion around the challenges of digital distractions and the quest to reclaim focus in today's interconnected world. Feel free to modify it to better align with the tone and themes of your book.

Chapter One

THE DIGITAL CHALLENGE

In an era where smartphones are omnipresent, social media feeds are ceaseless, and digital entertainment I Still a click away, today's teenagers find themselves entangled in a web of digital distractions. The pervasive influence of technology permeates every aspect of their lives, shaping their behaviors, perceptions, and priorities in profound ways. In "Teens Stolen Focus," we embark on a reflective journey into the heart of this digital dilemma, seeking to unravel its complexities and illuminate the challenges faced by adolescents in maintaining their focus amidst the cacophony of the digital age.
The central enigma of the digital dilemma is the paradoxical coexistence of connectivity and distraction. Undoubtedly, technology has facilitated unprecedented levels of connectivity among individuals. However, it has also caused a fragmentation of attention,

as individuals are perpetually reliant on their devices and subjected to an overwhelming avalanche of notifications, alerts, and stimuli. Teenagers, who are contending with the turbulent currents of digital technology, face an especially formidable task of sustaining concentration.

Digital distractions provide immediate gratification, amusement, and validation with the simple act of swiping a screen, which is an indisputable appeal. Social media platforms allure users with the prospect of establishing connections and a sense of belonging, whereas incessant streams of content vie for our focus, striving to capture a moment of our time. In our contemporary interconnected society, maintaining concentration has emerged as an invaluable asset—a talent that demands development in the face of an ocean of diversions.

However, in the midst of the cacophony of digital distractions, the repercussions of our shared diversion are progressively becoming more evident. Adolescents, whose cognitive development is especially vulnerable to the appeal of immediate gratification, are becoming ensnared in digital addiction. In the pursuit of online interaction, they are making sacrifices such as sleep, mental well-being, and interpersonal connections in the physical world. The consequences are far-reaching, affecting not only the individual but also the very structure of society.

Within educational settings, pupils contend with shortening attention spans and an unquenchable desire for multimedia stimulation. This necessitates that instructors modify their instructional approaches in order to captivate the transitory interest of their digitally savvy learners. Families contend within their households with the challenge of reconciling screen time with quality time, given the pervasive threat that technology poses to the integrity of familial connections. The emergence of cyberbullying and online torment within communities undermines the potential of digital connectivity, revealing the murky aspects of our excessively interconnected society. Without a doubt, let us further explore each of these facets:

In Classrooms:

The traditional model of education is facing unprecedented challenges in the digital age. Students, who are accustomed to the fast-paced, interactive nature of digital media, often struggle to maintain attention during traditional lectures or textbook-based lessons. The constant availability of smartphones and other digital devices exacerbates this issue, as students are tempted to multitask or seek entertainment during class time. As a result, educators are tasked with reimagining their teaching methods to engage digital-native learners better. This may involve incorporating interactive technologies, multimedia presentations, and hands-on activities that cater to different learning styles and capture students' fleeting attention spans. Additionally, educators must find ways to foster critical thinking skills and deep comprehension amidst the shallow distractions of the digital world.

In Homes:

Within the sanctuary of the home, families grapple with the delicate balance between screen time and quality time. The omnipresence of technology has transformed the dynamics of family life, as smartphones, tablets, and laptops vie for attention alongside traditional family activities. Parents are confronted with the challenge of setting boundaries around screen time and creating digital-free zones to protect precious moments of connection and intimacy. However, the allure of digital distractions can strain familial bonds, leading to diminished communication, decreased empathy, and a sense of disconnection among family members. Finding the right balance between technology use and meaningful human interaction becomes a constant struggle in the modern household.

In Communities:

The dark underbelly of cyberbullying and online harassment shadows the promise of digital connectivity. As social interactions increasingly migrate to digital platforms, teenagers are exposed to new forms of peer aggression and social pressure. Cyberbullying, characterized by the use of electronic communication to intimidate, threaten, or humiliate others, has become a pervasive issue in schools and communities worldwide. The anonymity and ubiquity of digital communication channels magnify the impact of cyberbullying, leaving victims feeling isolated, powerless, and vulnerable. , the rise of online harassment poses a threat to the inclusive and democratic ideals of digital connectivity, as marginalized individuals and communities are targeted with hate speech, discrimination, and online abuse. Addressing these challenges requires a concerted effort from parents, educators, policymakers, and technology companies to promote digital citizenship, foster empathy, and create safer online environments for all users.

In sum, the impact of digital distractions extends far beyond the individual, permeating classrooms, homes, and communities alike. By acknowledging and addressing these challenges, we can work towards creating a more balanced and mindful relationship with technology, one that fosters genuine connection, meaningful learning experiences, and a safer digital environment for all.

As we confront the realities of the digital dilemma, it becomes clear that reclaiming focus in the digital age is not merely a matter of individual willpower, but a collective endeavor that requires a fundamental shift in our relationship with technology. It calls for a reevaluation of our digital habits, a reimagining of our social norms, and a reaffirmation of our shared humanity in the face of digital distraction.

In the chapters that follow, we will delve deeper into the multifaceted dimensions of the digital dilemma, exploring its impact on mental health, education, social interactions, and beyond. Through introspection, dialogue, and action, we will seek to chart a course toward digital wellness, reclaiming our focus and forging meaningful connections amidst the cacophony of the digital age.

As we embark on this journey together, let us heed the call to reclaim our attention, reclaim our focus, and reclaim our humanity in a world where distraction has become the new normal. For it is only through mindful awareness and collective action that we can hope to navigate the digital labyrinth and emerge on the other side, empowered to thrive amidst the ever-changing currents of the digital age.

Chapter Two

THE IMPACT OF MENTAL HEALTH

In the digital age, where screens dominate our daily lives and virtual connections often supersede face-to-face interactions, the impact on mental health cannot be understated. In this chapter, we delve into the profound consequences of excessive screen time and digital engagement on the psychological well-being of today's teenagers.

The pervasive nature of smartphones and social media platforms has brought about significant changes to the developmental trajectory of adolescents, profoundly influencing aspects such as self-perception, social interactions, and emotional fortitude. The virtual world functions as a sanctuary and a battleground for numerous adolescents, providing them with an avenue to express themselves, find validation, and forge connections, while simultaneously subjecting them to an abundance of pressures, stresses, and dangers.

Throughout their entire lives, adolescents are fully engrossed in a digital environment where virtual interactions and real-life experiences are seamlessly interwoven. Adolescents utilize social media platforms such as Instagram, Snapchat, and TikTok as digital environments where they construct digital personas, share personal experiences, and establish connections with peers worldwide. Within the realm of digital platforms, not only is popularity determined by in-person engagements but also by metrics such as likes, remarks, and followers—a metric that can place significant strain on youthful individuals in search of affirmation and approval. The ubiquity of digital communication has resulted in a blurring of boundaries between the virtual and physical realms, generating an uninterrupted barrage of social stimuli that can evoke feelings of excitement and fatigue. The strain on contemporary adolescents to uphold a meticulously curated digital persona while simultaneously adapting to the perpetually evolving nature of social media can be overpowering. Occasions of missing out (FOMO) on the latest trends or social gatherings may induce compulsive notification monitoring and a pervasive anxiety regarding remaining connected and informed.

The proliferation of cyberbullying and online harassment has introduced an additional stratum of intricacy to the digital environment, subjecting adolescents to a variety of adverse encounters that may significantly impact their psychological well-being. From the protection of a digital screen, some users may be more inclined to partake in harmful actions that they would never contemplate attempting in person, which can result in instances of harassment, social exclusion, and emotional abuse. The heightened perception of distance and anonymity that characterize the digital realm can intensify the effects of cyberbullying, causing targets to experience feelings of isolation, susceptibility, and helplessness in the face of ceaseless cyber aggression. The emergence and pervasiveness of smartphones and social media platforms in the current digital era have brought about irrevocable changes to the realm of adolescent development. Although these technologies provide unparalleled prospects for interpersonal interaction, innovation, and the formation of communities, they also introduce novel pressures and stresses that may have detrimental effects on one's mental well-being. It is critical that, as we traverse the complexities of the digital age, we recognize the unique challenges that adolescents face today and collaborate to create a safer, more supportive online environment in which they can flourish and develop intellectually.

An extremely widespread consequence of digital technology on mental well-being is the amplification of emotions such as low self-esteem, comparison, and feelings of inadequacy. Social media platforms contribute to the perpetuation of exaggerated expectations and a perpetual sense of apprehension regarding one's own inaccessibility by curating feeds of idealized images and lifestyles. Adolescents, who are incessantly exposed to meticulously curated depictions of achievement and perfection, might succumb to emotions of insufficiency and uncertainty when they juxtapose their personal lives with the seemingly impeccable existences of their contemporaries.

The perpetual connectivity facilitated by smartphones and social media platforms has the potential to obscure the demarcation between the virtual and physical realms, resulting in compromised privacy, autonomy, and genuineness. Amidst the incessant digital din, adolescents who are inundated with notifications and alerts may find it difficult to disengage and find moments of solitude and reflection. The absence of leisure time can have detrimental effects on one's mental well-being, leading to increased levels of stress, anxiety, and exhaustion. The emergence of cyberbullying and online harassment has presented adolescents with novel mental health challenges. The ability to remain anonymous and at a distance through digital communication platforms may empower users to engage in harmful behaviors that they would be less likely to express in person. Individuals who fell prey to cyberbullying may confront significant psychological challenges, such as suicidal thoughts, anxiety, and melancholy, as they contend with the emotional repercussions of the abusive online environment.

In our capacities as policymakers, educators, and parents, it is critical that we acknowledge the convergence of digital technology and mental health concerns and adopt proactive measures to safeguard the overall welfare of contemporary adolescents. These initiatives encompass the promotion of digital literacy and resilience skills to assist adolescents in safely and responsibly navigating the online realm. Additionally, they aim to destigmatize discussions surrounding mental health concerns and encourage open dialogue.

We can establish a more conducive and

health-conscious setting for adolescents to flourish in the digital age by recognizing the influence of digital technology on mental well-being and collaborating to overcome these obstacles. Let us unite in our endeavor to give precedence to the welfare of our youth and guarantee that they are equipped with the necessary tools and resources to adeptly navigate the intricacies of the digital realm while maintaining fortitude, empathy, and introspection.

Chapter Three

EDUCATION IN THE DIGITAL AGE

In the rapidly evolving landscape of education, the integration of digital technology has become both a necessity and a challenge. As classrooms embrace the potential of digital tools and resources to enhance learning outcomes, educators are confronted with the task of navigating the complexities of the digital age while maintaining focus on their primary goal: fostering intellectual growth and academic achievement among their students.

In regards to learning, interacting, and engaging with educational content, the digital revolution has brought about a paradigm shift. Adolescents of the twenty-first century, who are often referred to as "digital natives," have been brought up during a period when information is readily accessible, interactive multimedia encounters are prevalent rather than traditional textbooks and e-readers, and such encounters are the norm rather than the exception. Amidst the current digital environment, the traditional educational model, which relied on lectures, textbooks, and memorization by rote, is being replaced by a more interactive and dynamic approach that harnesses the capabilities of technology to customize learning experiences and accommodate various learning preferences. Demonstrating access to resources and information is among the most substantial benefits that digital technology in education can offer. The advent of open educational resources, online learning platforms, and applications has provided students with unparalleled prospects to investigate unfamiliar topics, pursue areas of personal interest, and interact with learning materials in ways that were hitherto unimaginable. Digital tools possess the capacity to grant students access to interactive simulations, enable their participation in virtual classrooms, and facilitate collaboration on multimedia projects. By doing so, they enable students to embark on a transformative learning voyage and uncover novel avenues to knowledge.

Nevertheless, the potential of digital technology in education is accompanied by a multitude of obstacles and apprehensions. The digital divide—the disparity between those who have access to technology and those who do not—is among the most urgent problems. Although privileged students may possess cutting-edge technology and fast internet connections both inside and outside of school, disadvantaged students may struggle to obtain even the most fundamental technological tools, which would put them at a substantial disadvantage in the digital classroom. It is critical to bridge this digital divide in order to provide equal opportunities for all pupils to achieve success in the digital age.

Additionally, apprehensions have been expressed regarding the effects of the proliferation of digital technology in educational settings on students' cognitive development, critical thinking abilities, and attention spans. Students may encounter difficulties in sustaining concentration during conventional lectures or self-directed study periods due to the pervasive allure of digital diversions. Furthermore, the passive reception of information via digital screens can impede profound understanding and critical evaluation, resulting in a reliance on rote memorization and superficial learning rather than authentic comprehension.

In light of these obstacles, educators are obliged to reconsider their pedagogical strategies and teaching methodologies in order to seamlessly incorporate digital technology into the curriculum while simultaneously cultivating significant learning encounters for their pupils. Potential strategies to support students throughout their educational trajectory include the adoption of blended learning models that integrate both online and offline instruction, the implementation of project-based learning initiatives that foster collaboration and innovation, and the utilization of digital tools to deliver individualized feedback and assistance to pupils.

In order to effectively incorporate digital technology into the field of education, a methodical strategy is necessary that capitalizes on the capabilities of technology to improve academic achievements while safeguarding the fundamental values of interpersonal engagement, analytical reasoning, and inquisitiveness. By placing a premium on student-centered learning, promoting collaboration, and embracing innovation, educators can effectively navigate the challenges of the digital era and enable their pupils to flourish in a world that is becoming more interconnected and digitized.

Chapter Four

NAVIGATING SOCIAL INTERACTION

In the digital age, the landscape of social interactions among teenagers has undergone a profound transformation. While technology has provided unprecedented opportunities for connection and communication, it has also introduced new challenges and complexities to the social fabric of adolescence. In this chapter, we delve into the intricate dynamics of teenage social interactions in the digital age, exploring the impact of social media, online communities, and virtual communication on the formation of relationships and the development of social skills.

Adolescents utilize social media platforms as digital town squares to communicate, express themselves, and share personal experiences, as well as to establish connections with peers worldwide. Social media platforms such as Instagram, Snapchat, and TikTok provide an apparently boundless variety of possibilities for individuals to express themselves, find validation, and participate in social interactions. Nevertheless, an intricate web of social dynamics lurks beneath the veneer of curated feeds and filtered images, wherein the metrics of influence, status, and popularity are quantified in terms of followers, likes, and remarks.

Social media platforms provide a valuable resource and a source of distress for numerous adolescents. While they enable them to communicate with others and feel a sense of belonging, they also subject them to the detrimental influences of comparison, seeking validation, and online scrutiny. A culture of performative behavior can result from the desire for social acceptability and validation; adolescents may feel obligated to present an idealized version of themselves online to gain the approval and likes of their peers. Adolescents may experience mental health consequences as a result of this never-ending cycle of seeking validation; they may develop feelings of inadequacy, self-doubt, and anxiety as they navigate the intricate landscape of virtual social networks.

The influence of social media on the dynamics of friendship and intimacy among adolescents has been profound, erasing the distinction between offline and online interactions. Although digital connections provide advantages such as instantaneous communication and virtual companionship, they may also undermine the genuineness and profundity of in-person relationships. Adolescents who have become acclimated to utilizing electronic devices for communication may encounter difficulties in cultivating the essential social competencies required to establish substantial interpersonal relationships in physical environments. Consequently, this can result in feelings of isolation, loneliness, and detachment.

Additionally, adolescents must navigate the complexities of digital subcultures and online communities, where identities, values, and shared interests converge in virtual spaces. Online communities, including fandoms, gaming communities, and specialist interest groups, provide adolescents with a sense of camaraderie and belonging. However, they may also subject them to the dangers of cyberharassment, noxious behavior, and cyberbullying. In addition to digital literacy and the ability to think critically, navigating the complexities of online communities demands fortitude in the face of hostility and negativity.

In the digital age, we must assist adolescents in navigating the complexities of social interactions. These encompass encouraging discourse regarding the advantages and disadvantages of social media, advocating for responsible online conduct and digital citizenship, and furnishing assistance and direction to aid adolescents in cultivating sound interpersonal connections and communication capabilities in the digital and physical realms.

In essence, by cultivating qualities such as authenticity, resilience, and empathy in our digital exchanges, we can establish a more comprehensive and encouraging virtual milieu that facilitates the social, emotional, and psychological development of adolescents during the digital era. By utilizing technology in a conscientious and collaborative manner, we can enhance our social bonds, develop a more profound comprehension of ourselves and others, and establish a society that is more interconnected and empathetic for future generations.

Chapter Five

REDISCOVERING FOCUS

In a world inundated with digital distractions and constant stimuli, the ability to maintain focus has become a precious commodity, particularly for teenagers navigating the complexities of adolescence in the digital age. In this chapter, we explore the importance of reclaiming focus amidst the cacophony of the modern world and delve into practical strategies for fostering mindfulness, concentration, and presence in the midst of digital distractions.

The ubiquitous nature of smartphones, social media, and digital entertainment has profoundly altered adolescents' interactions with the world. Consequently, this has frequently resulted in fragmented attention spans and a reduced ability to maintain sustained focus. Adolescents are perpetually confronted with diversions that tear them from the present and fragment their focus, including the allure of limitless perusing on social media, the temptation of binge-watching television programs, and the constant ping of notifications from smartphones.

However, in the midst of the disorder caused by digital diversions, adolescents have the potential to regain their concentration and develop a more profound sense of mindfulness and consciousness. Through the promotion of mindfulness—the deliberate and accepting observation of the current moment—adolescents have the potential to develop a state of tranquility in the face of the inundation of digital stimuli and reclaim authority over their mental health and focus. The act of practicing mindfulness entails developing an attentiveness to one's current thoughts, emotions, and sensations, devoid of any evaluative or emotional attachment. Teenagers can develop greater clarity, focus, and resilience in the face of digital distractions by anchoring their attention in the present moment through the use of techniques such as mindful movement, body scan meditation, and mindful breathing.

To cultivate focus and concentration, one must establish settings that are conducive to uninterrupted concentration and in-depth work. Possible strategies include implementing restrictions on screen usage, designating specific areas within the household as "tech-free zones," and establishing daily schedules that emphasize periods of concentrated effort and deliberate relaxation. Adolescents can maximize their cognitive performance and strengthen their capacity to profoundly engage with meaningful tasks and activities by minimizing distractions and establishing environments that promote concentration.

Additionally, developing the practices of deliberate goal-setting, time management, and prioritization can be advantageous for adolescents. Teenagers can optimize their productivity in the digital age by establishing explicit objectives, decomposing tasks into feasible components, and scheduling dedicated periods for concentrated effort. Instilling adolescents with a sense of purpose and meaning can serve as a potent incentive for them to maintain concentration and involvement in their endeavors. Adolescents who possess a sense of purpose can remain rooted in matters that genuinely concern them amidst the distractions of the digital world, whether it be fostering meaningful relationships, pursuing a passion, or contributing to a cause in which they believe. In the digital age, reclaiming focus entails more than mere productivity optimization and distraction management; it also necessitates reclaiming our agency, presence, and capacity for profound engagement with the surrounding world. Adolescents have the potential to rediscover the pleasure of being completely present in that which truly matters by promoting mindfulness, establishing nurturing environments, and developing habits of intentionality and purpose.

Chapter Six

EMPOWERING CHANGE

In the midst of the digital revolution, where screens dominate our daily lives and virtual connections often supersede face-to-face interactions, the imperative to reclaim focus and foster digital wellness has never been more pressing. In this chapter, we explore the power of collective action and individual agency in navigating the complexities of the digital age, empowering teenagers to take control of their digital lives and forge a path toward greater balance, resilience, and well-being.

Fundamentally, in order to promote digital wellness and regain concentration, a paradigm shift is necessary—a reassessment of our connection with technology and a dedication to placing human connection, presence, and authenticity at the forefront of our lives amidst a digitally saturated environment. By recognizing the influence that digital technology has on our daily lives and adopting the practice of mindful awareness, we can initiate the process of reclaiming control over our attention and fostering a more deliberate and equitable approach to utilizing technology.

By furnishing adolescents with the requisite knowledge, abilities, and materials to securely and responsibly navigate the intricacies of the digital era, education is among the most influential instruments in fostering transformation. These encompass initiatives that foster digital literacy, media literacy, and critical thinking in order to assist adolescents in differentiating between fact and fiction, avoiding online dangers, and determining their digital conduct with knowledge. We can foster a more secure and encouraging online environment for all by providing adolescents with the necessary resources to boldly and resiliently navigate the digital terrain.

Promoting constructive discourse and correspondence is critical for enabling adolescents to confront the obstacles of the digital era. Facilitating open dialogues regarding the advantages and disadvantages of technology can assist adolescents in cultivating a heightened consciousness regarding their digital behaviors, acknowledging the detrimental effects of digital diversions on their overall welfare, and investigating approaches to reestablish equilibrium and concentration in their lives. We can dismantle the obstacles that discourage adolescents from seeking assistance and support when they are in need by cultivating an environment that promotes transparency, compassion, and welfare.

Promoting collaboration and community engagement is critical in addition to education and communication, for enabling adolescents to effect positive change in their digital lives and communities. Teenagers can effectively utilize peer support, mentorship, and collective action to generate spaces for connection, creativity, and meaningful engagement in the digital realm, amplify their voices, and advocate for change. Teens possess the ability to mold the future of the digital environment and establish a more equitable and compassionate digital society for future generations through initiatives such as coordinating digital detox challenges, establishing peer support groups, and advocating for policies that promote digital wellness.

Individual action is insufficient to effect change in the digital age; collective action and shared responsibility are required. We can build a world in which adolescents can flourish intellectually, emotionally, and socially in the digital age by collaborating to promote digital literacy, encourage open dialogue, and establish supportive communities. By utilizing the transformative potential of technology and cultivating mindful awareness, it is possible to enhance every aspect of life, foster more profound connections, and establish a society that is more compassionate and equitable for every individual.

Chapter Seven

THE ROLE OF PARENTING IN THE DIGITAL AGE

In the rapidly evolving landscape of the digital age, parents play a crucial role in guiding and supporting their teenagers through the challenges and opportunities presented by technology. In this chapter, we delve into the complex dynamics of parenting in the digital age, exploring the influence of parental guidance and supervision on teenagers' digital habits, well-being, and development of focus and resilience amidst digital distractions.

Parents, being the principal providers of care and exemplars in their children's lives, possess a substantial impact on the values, attitudes, and conduct of their adolescents, including their technological engagement. In a time when smartphones are ubiquitous and social media influences all facets of existence, parents must find a way to protect their adolescents' well-being amidst the pervasive influence of digital diversions while simultaneously embracing the advantages of technology.

In the digital age, parents assume a critical role as educators and mentors, imparting their adolescents with the requisite knowledge, abilities, and principles to securely and responsibly navigate the intricate realm of the Internet. This includes fostering media literacy, critical thinking, and digital literacy in order to assist adolescents in differentiating fact from fiction, identifying online dangers, and making informed decisions regarding their digital behavior. Parents can help adolescents feel empowered to inquire, seek advice, and make responsible decisions regarding their digital lives by encouraging open dialogue and communication regarding the advantages and disadvantages of technology.

Moreover, parents shape the digital habits and priorities of their adolescents by acting as gatekeepers and role models. Parents can assist adolescents in developing balanced lives and healthy digital behaviors by establishing clear boundaries around screen time and demonstrating mindful technology usage. This may entail establishing restrictions on the usage of electronic devices, designating areas within the household free from technology, and giving precedence to in-person conversations and quality time spent with family. Parents can enable their adolescents to flourish intellectually, emotionally, and socially in the digital age by cultivating a household culture that values intentionality, presence, and connection.

In addition, parents have an essential responsibility to provide support for the mental health and overall well-being of their adolescents in the face of the difficulties and pressures that accompany the digital era. Parents can assist their adolescents in handling the pressures of digital distractions, peer pressure, and online negativity with composure and fortitude by encouraging self-care, empathy, and resilience. This may entail fostering constructive self-dialogue, encouraging the adoption of healthy coping mechanisms, and organizing offline activities that facilitate meaningful connection, creative expression, and physical activity. Parental involvement in their adolescents' mental and emotional health can assist them in developing the fortitude and resiliency required to succeed despite the difficulties posed by digital technologies.

Parenting in the digital age ultimately necessitates a comprehensive strategy that harmonizes direction, assistance, and empowerment. Parents can assist their adolescents in navigating the turbulent digital environment with fortitude and assurance by encouraging candid dialogue, establishing explicit criteria, and exemplifying appropriate digital conduct. Adolescents can cultivate the necessary competencies, principles, and fortitude to flourish intellectually, emotionally, and socially in the era of digital technology within a nurturing and supportive milieu established by parents via conscientious parenting and practical parenting.

Chapter Eight

SHAPING THE FUTURE

We reflect on the journey we've embarked upon—a journey to understand, navigate, and thrive in the digital age. As we stand at the threshold of the future, poised on the precipice of endless possibilities and unforeseen challenges, we are confronted with a profound question: How do we shape the future of the digital landscape, ensuring that it is one characterized by balance, compassion, and human flourishing?

Influencing the trajectory of the digital era necessitates a shared dedication to cultivating digital wellness—a comprehensive methodology towards technology utilization that places emphasis on meaningful participation, connection, and overall well-being within the digital realm. This requires recognizing the limitations and drawbacks of technology while reimagining our relationship with it, while also recognizing its potential as a tool for empowerment, creativity, and connection. Through the adoption of a societal framework that values mindfulness, intentionality, and empathy, it is possible to utilize the revolutionary capabilities of technology in order to establish a realm in which success is ultimately determined by the well-being of individuals.

A fundamental aspect in influencing the trajectory of the digital era is the advocacy for universal digital literacy and empowerment. This entails the following: facilitating equal opportunities for accessing technology and digital resources; advocating for principles of inclusive and accessible design; and enabling people of all ages and backgrounds to utilize technology in a way that improves their communities and lives. By advocating for equal access to technology and cultivating digital literacy, it is possible to narrow the digital divide and establish a digital society that is more inclusive and participatory for every individual.

Furthermore, in order to influence the trajectory of the digital era, it is imperative to cultivate digital citizenship—a collection of principles, competencies, and obligations that enable individuals to participate in the digital realm in a conscientious and morally upright manner. It encompasses the following: advocating for digital rights and privacy protections; challenging detrimental norms and behaviors that sustain discrimination, harassment, and exclusion in the online sphere; and fostering empathy, respect, and civility in online interactions. We can create safer, more inclusive online communities where individuals can connect, collaborate, and flourish without fear, harassment, or discrimination by promoting a culture of digital citizenship.

Moreover, in order to influence the trajectory of the digital age, one must be dedicated to cultivating ingenuity and novelty within the digital domain. By embracing an interdisciplinary approach that incorporates inquisitiveness, originality, and progress, we can leverage the profound capabilities of technology to tackle critical issues that confront our species, including but not limited to social justice, healthcare, climate change, and education.

In order to truly influence the trajectory of the digital age, it is imperative that all stakeholders contribute. This entails a concerted effort to cultivate digital wellness, advocate for digital literacy and empowerment, nurture digital citizenship, and support innovation and creativity within the digital domain. Through collective efforts to foster a digital culture that is more conscientious, inclusive, and humane, it is possible to envision a future in which technology functions as a positive influence, enhancing our existence, fortifying our communities, and enabling us to construct a world that is fair, environmentally conscious, and sustainable for future generations.

Chapter Nine

EMBRACING DIGITAL WELL-BEING

As we navigate the complexities of the digital landscape, it becomes increasingly clear that fostering digital well-being is not just a personal responsibility but a collective endeavor that requires mindfulness, intentionality, and compassion.

Digital well-being pertains to the pursuit of equilibrium in our association with technology—acknowledging both its potential to enhance our existence and its capacity to inundate and engulf us when not reined in. It is about fostering consciousness regarding our digital behaviors and their influence on our holistic welfare, as well as deliberately selecting our technological interactions in a way that improves our quality of life rather than diminishes it.

A fundamental element of digital well-being entails the development of mindfulness, which entails the intentional and receptive observation of the current moment with an attitude of acceptance and inquiry. Through cultivating mindfulness regarding our digital behaviors, cognitions, and sentiments, we can fortify our capacity for concentration, clarity, and fortitude when confronted with digital diversions. Engaging in mindfulness practices, including meditation, mindful breathing, and digital detoxes, can assist individuals in reclaiming control over their attention and mental health while navigating the chaotic digital environment.

Furthermore, the concept of digital well-being pertains to the cultivation of significant relationships within the digital domain—ones that provide nourishment and support instead of depletion or exhaustion. By fostering genuine connections and cultivating a sense of belonging in the digital realm, we can cultivate a greater sense of fulfillment and well-being in our digital lives and counteract feelings of loneliness, isolation, and disconnection.

Moreover, the promotion of resilience and self-care in the midst of digital obstacles and setbacks constitutes digital well-being. These include prioritizing self-care practices that nourish and replenish us, establishing realistic goals and expectations for our digital lives, and cultivating healthy coping mechanisms to manage tension, anxiety, and digital overload. By placing our mental, emotional, and physical well-being first in the digital domain, we can develop the fortitude and fortitude necessary to gracefully and ethically navigate the complexities of the digital age. In essence, the concept of embracing digital well-being pertains to reclaiming control over one's digital existence by consciously determining how technology can be utilized to enhance one's life and promote personal growth. By placing emphasis on resilience and self-care, nurturing meaningful connections, and cultivating mindfulness, it is possible to establish a more harmonious and satisfying rapport with technology. Such a relationship would enrich our lives, fortify our interpersonal connections, and enable us to flourish not only in the current digital era but also in the future. By cultivating deliberate intention and maintaining a state of mindful awareness, it is possible to adopt digital well-being as a fundamental value that directs our technological interactions, guaranteeing that they facilitate development, connection, and success in the era of digitalization and beyond.

Chapter Ten

A VISION FOR THE FUTURE

As we conclude our journey through the complexities of the digital age, we cast our gaze toward the horizon and envision a future where technology serves as a force for promising—a future where digital innovation is guided by principles of ethics, equity, and empathy, and where all share the benefits of technology.

We present a concluding chapter wherein we delineate a vision for the future of the digital environment—a vision distinguished by cooperation, ingenuity, and the advancement of humanity. Fundamental to this ideology is a steadfast dedication to utilizing the paradigm-shifting capabilities of technology in order to tackle critical issues that confront our species, including but not limited to climate change, healthcare, education, and social justice.

A commitment to digital equity and inclusion is fundamental to our future vision—a future in which the availability of technology and digital resources is not considered a privilege but rather an inherent right. This initiative aims to eliminate the digital divide by providing affordable devices, equitable access to high-speed internet, and digital literacy education for all communities, with a particular focus on historically marginalized or underserved populations. We can ensure that future generations reside in a more just, equitable, and inclusive world by enabling people of all backgrounds to actively engage in the digital economy and society. Furthermore, our forward-thinking perspective is firmly rooted in ethical technology principles. A technological future is characterized by the prioritization of human well-being, autonomy, and dignity in its design and deployment. Digital governance encompasses several key objectives: fostering accountability and transparency throughout the technological design and development process, protecting digital privacy and security, and alleviating the adverse effects of technology on social cohesion, mental health, and democratic governance. By advocating for ethical standards and practices within the digital industry, it is possible to guarantee that technology functions as a mechanism that promotes liberation, empowerment, and social welfare.

Moreover, our prospective outlook encompasses the profound capacity for digital innovation to bring about significant changes—a future in which technology is utilized to tackle among the most urgent issues that confront the human race. It entails capitalizing on the potential of emergent technologies, including biotechnology, artificial intelligence, and renewable energy, to effect positive social and environmental change through research and development expenditures. By cultivating an environment that encourages entrepreneurialism and innovation in the digital realm, we can discover fresh avenues towards universal prosperity, sustainability, and welfare.
In essence, our aspiration for the future is

marked by optimism, hope, and potentiality—
a future in which technology functions as a
means to facilitate human flourishing,
connection, and empowerment. Through
collective efforts to foster a digital culture
that is more conscientious, inclusive, and
humane, it is possible to establish a future in
which technology functions as a positive
influence, enhancing our existence, fortifying
our communities, and enabling us to construct
a future world that is more equitable,
sustainable, and fair for future generations.
By means of combined endeavors and
conscientious cognizance, it is possible to
mold a forthcoming era in which the digital
age's potential is completely actualized and
wherein all individuals benefit from
technological advancements.

About the Author

Gbogo .S. Adegboye is a multifaceted professional, serving as a manager, business economist, entrepreneur, and motivational speaker across Africa. Adegboye boasts bachelor's degrees from Yale University, IPMA, and Adonai University, along with a Master of Business Administration (MBA) from Salfold University, Manchester. While born in South Africa, he currently resides in Nigeria, actively engaging as a motivational speaker in various institutions, industries, and seminars, particularly catering to young and aspiring managers throughout the African continent.

Acknowledgment

To begin with, I give all the credit to God for the effective culmination of this medical composition. Without the guidance of God, who has been a constant aid and sustainer and whose wisdom enabled the successful completion of this medical manuscript, it would have been unattainable. Additionally, I would like to extend my gratitude to my family, friends, well-wishers, and numerous others whom I am unable to name here, as they have consistently supported me in some capacity from the inception to the completion of this manuscript.

THANKS FOR READING

www.ingramcontent.com/pod-product-compliance
Lightning Source LLC
Chambersburg PA
CBHW051244120626
46547CB00014B/1785